BUILT FOR SUCCESS

THE STORY OF

eBay

First published in the UK in 2013 by
Franklin Watts
338 Euston Road
London NW1 3BH

Franklin Watts Australia
Level 17/207 Kent Street
Sydney, NSW 2000

First published by Creative Education,
an imprint of The Creative Company.
www.thecreativecompany.us

A CIP catalogue record for this book is available from the
British Library.

ISBN: 978 1 4451 2100 0

Dewey number: 381.1'77

Printed in China

Franklin Watts is a division of
Hachette Children's Books,
an Hachette UK company.

www.hachette.co.uk

DESIGN BY **ZENO DESIGN**
ART DIRECTION BY **RITA MARSHALL**

PHOTOGRAPHS BY Alamy (ICP, Gina Kelly, Gary Lucken,
NetPhotos, SiliconValleyStock, Varioimages GmbH & Co.
KG), Corbis (Kim Kulish, Julian Stratenschulte/dpa, Kimberly
White/Reuters), Getty Images (Daniel Acker/Bloomberg, Tony
Avelar/Bloomberg, Vince Bucci, William Thomas Cain, Check
Six, Mikel Laburu/Bloomberg, Michael Loccisano, David
McNew, Jason Merritt, Jb Reed/Bloomberg, Kurt Vinion, James
D. Wilson/Liaison Agency)

BUILT FOR SUCCESS

THE STORY OF

eBay

W

FRANKLIN WATTS
LONDON • SYDNEY

SARA GILBERT

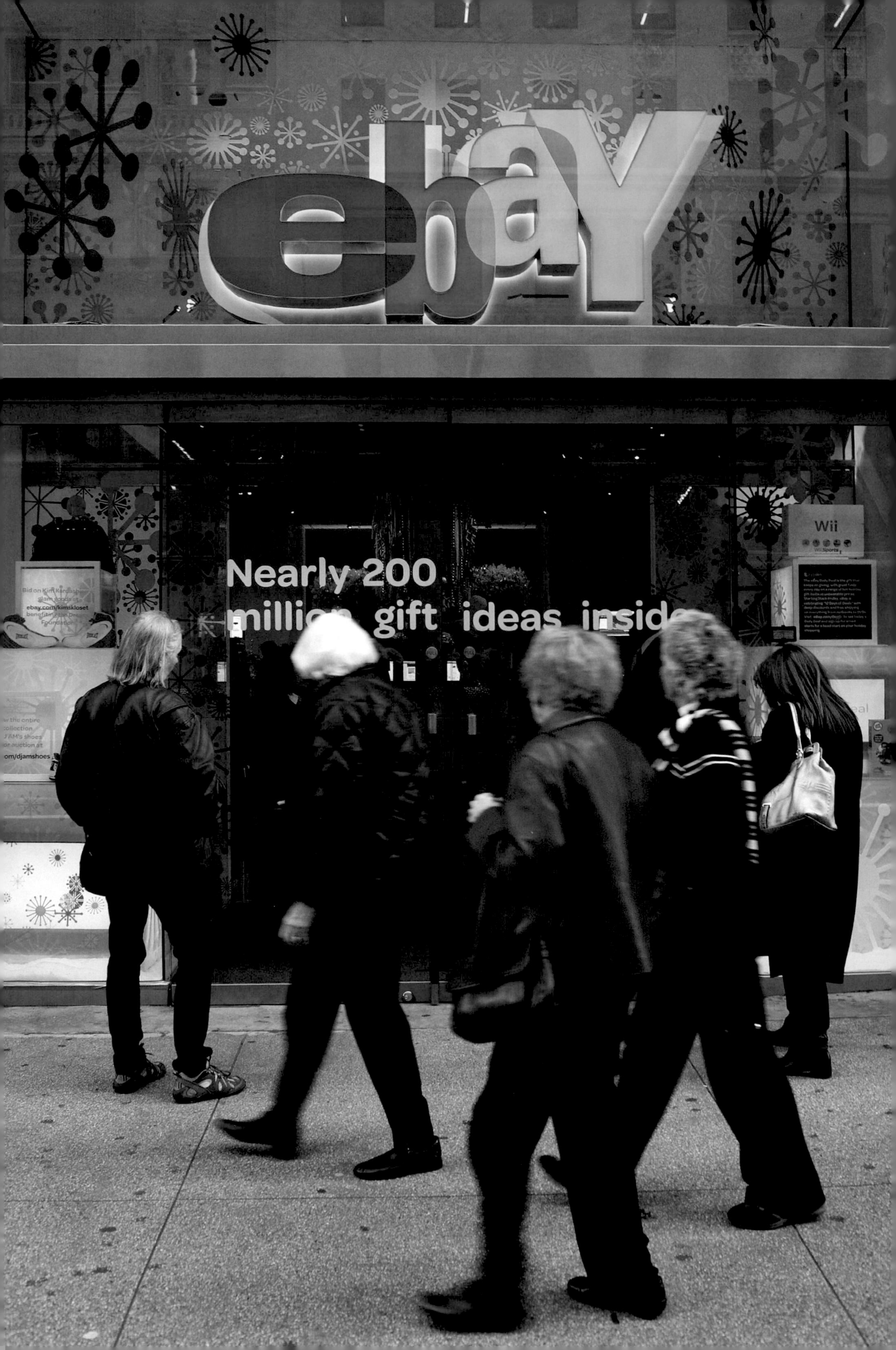
ebay
Nearly 200
million gift ideas inside
Wii

P ierre Omidyar had bought the laser pointer on a whim. He used it to play with his cat for two weeks, then discovered it didn't work anymore. But instead of chucking it out, he decided to use it as an experiment. In autumn 1995, Omidyar listed it on AuctionWeb, a new part of his personal web page, under the heading 'Broken Laser Pointer'. A week went by without any interest. But then bids started coming in. When the two-week auction period ended, Omidyar was surprised to see that someone had bid £9.27 for something that didn't work. He contacted the buyer to make sure he understood it was broken. "I'm a collector of broken laser pointers," the man replied. Omidyar packed it up, posted it and completed his first online auction sale.

CHAPTER ONE

Start the bidding

On a Friday afternoon in 1995, Pierre Omidyar planted himself in the office of his home in Campbell, California. Omidyar, a 28-year-old software engineer, had decided to spend the US Labor Day bank holiday weekend creating the perfect online marketplace – a venue where buyers and sellers could connect directly, and, through the process of bidding, agree upon an appropriate price for an item.

In four days, he finished designing a rather stark, grey-coloured, text-heavy website that would host online auctions for free. Then he posted a note about his new site – which he called AuctionWeb – on a pair of online announcement sites.

After a few days, listings for non-computer-related items such as a metal Superman lunch box and an autographed Michael Jackson poster showed up. Within a week, more than 30 items had been listed. By the end of the year, AuctionWeb had hosted thousands of auctions, attracting more than 10,000 bids in total.

At first, Omidyar offered the auction service for free on his own website – www. ebay.com, which also hosted a home page for the small biotechnology firm where his fiancée worked, a home page for a group of people his fiancée went to

Pierre Omidyar was born in France to Iranian parents; the family moved to America six years later

university with, and another section Omidyar had created to distribute information about the Ebola virus, a devastating disease in which he had taken a particular interest. The site ran from his personal account with a local **Internet service provider** called Best. But in February 1996, Best **administrators** noticed that the volume of traffic on AuctionWeb was slowing its system, and began charging Omidyar the business rate of $250 (£156) a month. "That's when I said, 'You know, this is kind of a fun hobby, but $250 a month is a lot of money,'" Omidyar later recalled.

To keep the service running Omidyar implemented a fee of 5 per cent of the sale price for items under $25 (£16) and 2.5 per cent on items that sold for more. He didn't send out bills, and didn't immediately set up a system to verify that all sellers paid the fee, choosing to believe that most people were honest enough to follow through on their own. Soon his mailbox was stuffed with envelopes containing cheques, cash and even coins taped to index cards. After a month of charging for the service he had earned over $250 (£156).

In March, revenues soared to £625, and in April they went up to £1,560. In May, over £3,125 arrived, and Omidyar – who was still working full-time at a mobile communications company called General Magic – could no longer keep up with all the paperwork. He hired a friend, Chris Agarpao, to help open envelopes. But when revenues topped £6,250 in June, Omidyar quit his job and made AuctionWeb a real business.

Omidyar spent most of his time maintaining the site's **server**, writing **codes** for new features, and fielding emails from users who had a disagreement with a buyer or seller on the site. Omidyar's standard answer was, "You guys work it out", and usually the two parties did. But he realised that he needed a formal system to ensure good customer service amongst users. So he set up the Feedback Forum, an online bulletin board where buyers and sellers could vent their frustrations, deal with disagreements and communicate with Omidyar. Meanwhile, Omidyar also knew he needed help turning AuctionWeb

Part of eBay's initial appeal was its simple, colourful presentation and easily navigable website

into a fully fledged business, so earlier that year he had turned to Jeff Skoll, a friend who had already founded two high-tech companies. Omidyar saw Skoll's **entrepreneurial** experience as a complement to his own technological cleverness, and asked him to do some consulting work on a part-time basis.

One of Skoll's first tasks was to find an office space for the company, which was still operating out of Omidyar's house. He located a small suite in Campbell that he, Omidyar and Agarpao moved into during the summer of 1996, when Skoll became a full-time employee and the company's first president [head]. They set up cheap desks, a folding table and beach chairs. Then they began hiring people to help develop the business and meet the needs of the site's users. Skoll asked two frequent posters to the Feedback Forum to handle customer-support questions from their home computers. Then he brought in Mary Lou Song as **public relations** manager.

By autumn 1996, AuctionWeb was hosting approximately 28,000 auctions each month, charging a small listing fee for each of them (a cost that frequent users had actually asked for in order to keep the site from being cluttered by junk). The most popular items on the site were Beanie Babies – small stuffed animals that were systematically being 'retired' by the toymaker Ty. In 1997, sellers on AuctionWeb made roughly £312,500 on Beanie Babies – 6.6 per cent of the site's total sales.

The Beanie Babies craze helped fuel AuctionWeb's growth in 1997 – but it wasn't the only factor. Interest in the Internet as a whole was increasing; in spring 1996, fewer than 19 million people in the United States and Canada were using it, but, by December, more than 50 million people were active online and 341,000 were using eBay. In January 1997, AuctionWeb hosted 200,000 auctions. Later in the year, it marked the sale of its millionth item: a Sesame Street Big Bird toy. The first few months of 1997 soon became known as the Great eBay Flood – the website itself became known simply as eBay, because it had pushed everything else off Omidyar's site.

> "What I wanted to do was create an efficient market, where regular people could compete with big business... It was a little bit of an experiment."
>
> EBAY FOUNDER PIERRE OMIDYAR

Jeff Skoll was brought up and educated in Canada before moving to California, where he met Omidyar

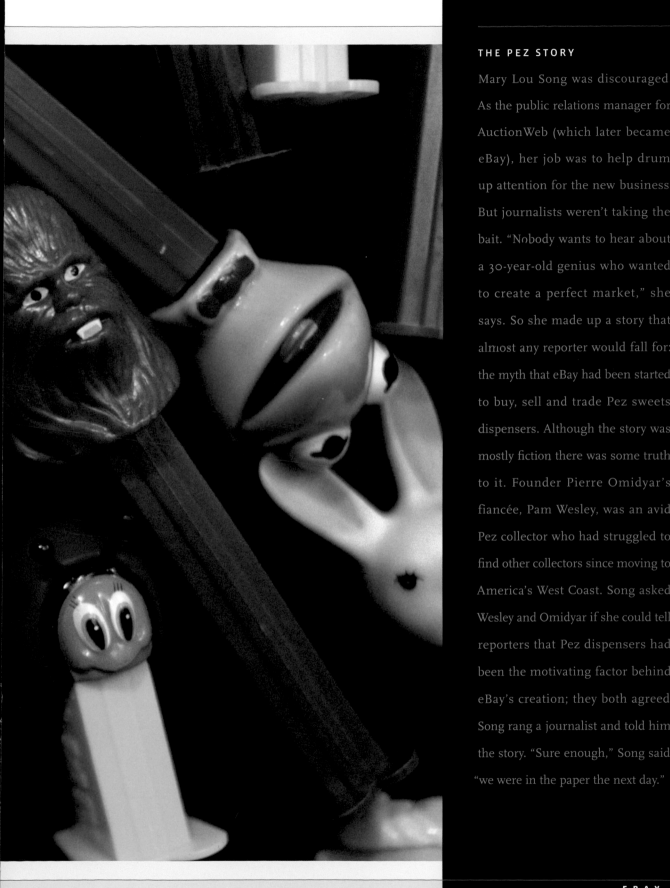

THE PEZ STORY

Mary Lou Song was discouraged. As the public relations manager for AuctionWeb (which later became eBay), her job was to help drum up attention for the new business. But journalists weren't taking the bait. "Nobody wants to hear about a 30-year-old genius who wanted to create a perfect market," she says. So she made up a story that almost any reporter would fall for: the myth that eBay had been started to buy, sell and trade Pez sweets dispensers. Although the story was mostly fiction there was some truth to it. Founder Pierre Omidyar's fiancée, Pam Wesley, was an avid Pez collector who had struggled to find other collectors since moving to America's West Coast. Song asked Wesley and Omidyar if she could tell reporters that Pez dispensers had been the motivating factor behind eBay's creation; they both agreed. Song rang a journalist and told him the story. "Sure enough," Song said, "we were in the paper the next day."

CHAPTER TWO

Meeting Meg

In the midst of the Great eBay Flood, Omidyar started thinking about hiring a new chief **executive** officer (CEO) to oversee eBay's operations. He and Skoll recognised that while they brought technological expertise and entrepreneurial spirit to the organization, neither of them had the business background to keep the company growing.

So when Benchmark Capital, a company that invested money in **start-ups** that showed potential for great growth, put £3.12 million into eBay's development they decided it was time to bring in a CEO.

In February 1998, Meg Whitman was hired to lead the company; Omidyar became chairman while Skoll became the vice president of **strategic planning** and analysis. Whitman's CV included high-level jobs with Proctor & Gamble and Disney, as well as her most recent position as the general manager of toymaker Hasbro's preschool division. However, she had little experience with the Internet, and received a cool welcome from many of eBay's 30 employees, who maintained a casual culture at the office, wearing jeans or shorts to work, and considered Whitman's US East Coast corporate background un-'eBaysian'.

Despite the doubts of some people, Whitman's background proved essential that September as eBay prepared to offer **shares** in the company to the public. EBay was eager to raise additional funds from investors – but more importantly, Omidyar wanted to establish the eBay **brand** and bring it the attention he felt it deserved in the business community. "No one was paying attention to us," he explained. "If we take the company public, it will be a lot easier to get the word out."

The company was already well known to the growing number of collectors and online shoppers using the site, as it was one of only a handful of **e-commerce** sites doing business on the web at the time. On 30 June, eBay officially registered its one-millionth user. But while eBay's numbers were riding high, the stock market was tumbling. On 31 August, the stock market experienced its second-largest drop to that point in history.

Despite the uncertainty of the market eBay's **stock** sold well. It was expected to be offered for £11.25 a share, but instead sold for £33.30. By the end of the first day, eBay had sold 3.5 million shares and raised £39.4 million. Back at company headquarters (now in San Jose), eBay's approximately 75 employees, many of whom had **stock options** and were now quite wealthy, celebrated by queuing up and dancing from floor to floor until another tenant in the building called security personnel.

With the sale of eBay's stock, Omidyar, Skoll and Whitman all became instant millionaires. But they tried to maintain the same low-key culture that had always defined the business. Omidyar still wore his hair in a ponytail, and drove his beat-up Volkswagen Cabriolet to work; Skoll, who still lived in a rental house with a group of friends, showed up in a 10-year-old Mazda RX-7. When they moved into a larger building later that year they decided not to build luxurious offices, instead designing work cubicles for everyone – even for Whitman and Omidyar.

Cool necklace, thank yo

Mens/boys skull/pirate g

 Goods arrived quickly, m

> "What is really interesting about eBay is that … it is the users who build the company. They bring the product to the site, they merchandise the product, and they distribute it once sold."
>
> MEG WHITMAN, FORMER CEO OF EBAY

Through Finger. An

 Fab item. Fast Delivery.

Pretty bag/mobile phone

 Lovely item. Fast Deliver

By emphasising user feedback, eBay created a business in which customers largely policed themselves

One of the reasons eBay had been so successful was the relationship it had developed with its 'community', the company's term for its regular buyers and sellers. Omidyar had based the company on the belief that most people were basically good, which drove the relatively hands-off approach eBay staff took with most auctions. And if the site was considering a change of any significance, it discussed the issue with users via its popular online bulletin boards.

But in February 1999, eBay management announced that it was banning guns and ammunition from the site, as it was too hard for the company to make sure buyers met the legal requirements for purchasing a gun. Even users who supported the regulation protested the fact that they had not been consulted or warned about the change in advance. They worried that eBay was breaking away from its community-based roots and becoming a more corporate entity. Whitman understood their complaints: although she didn't reverse the new rule, she learned to communicate with users before announcing changes.

As the gun ban fiasco was dying down an even bigger problem arose. Just before 7.00am on 10 June 1999, eBay's site went down. Although outages happened regularly, they usually didn't last more than a few hours. But this time it took 22 hours to get eBay back up and running. As engineers struggled to correct the issue, staff taped sheets of brown paper over the windows to shield themselves from television cameras and reporters hoping to learn what the problem was. Whitman, meanwhile, fielded emails and message-board posts from frustrated users, including many full-time sellers who depended on eBay for their income. At a staff meeting the next morning, she asked, "How are we going to make it up to them?" Her decision was to refund all fees for each of the more than two million auctions that were active during the outage.

This decision cost eBay almost £3.12 million. The company's stock prices also dropped in the aftermath of the outage. But two days after the site was back online, eBay registered almost 25,000 new users and saw bids increase by 13 per cent.

BUILT ON BEANIE BABIES

Chicago-based toy manufacturer Ty introduced the first Beanie Babies – small stuffed animals with sweet names – in 1993. Three years later, it started retiring them one by one, which meant that those specific products were no longer being made. As the adorable animals became harder to find, collectors across the country turned to a new website that allowed them to buy or sell them online: eBay (then known as AuctionWeb). So many Beanie Babies were listed on eBay that, in April 1997, they were given their own category; this category quickly ranked first in the number of items sold. In May 1997, £312,500 worth of Beanie Babies sold on eBay, at an average price of over £20 each (their original retail price was £3). This accounted for over six per cent of the site's total sales volume. The tiny toys are still popular on eBay; in 2013, more than 70,000 Beanie Babies were listed on the US site.

CHAPTER THREE

Growing pains

EBay started the new decade with a bit of good publicity: it had become the number one e-commerce site, doing more business than any other retail site, including Amazon. But this didn't make the online auction site any more comfortable about the competitors creeping into its territory.

Yahoo! auctions had gone live just days before eBay offered its stock to the public, and Amazon had launched its own site, Amazon Auction, late in 1999. Neither had made a serious dent in eBay's business, but Whitman was nervous nonetheless.

This is why she and the rest of eBay took note when a young entrepreneur in US state of Pennsylvania started Half.com, a site where used, mass-produced items were sold for no more than half of their list price. Whitman recognised that the site was well crafted and that the option to buy used films, books, music and games at a fixed price would be attractive to online bargain hunters. She also recognised that eBay didn't have time to build a rival site of its own. So in June 2000 – just six months after Half.com was launched – eBay bought the site for 5 million shares of its own stock, which was worth about £212 million. "Half.com's fixed-price format complements eBay's current business by giving our existing users new choices for trading," Whitman said when the deal closed.

half.com
an eBay company

Search:

Books

Audiobooks
Fiction
Top 200
$0.99 or less
Sell Books

Movies

Home

Music

World Music
Soundtracks
Top 200
$2.99 or less
Sell Music

Games

PS2
Xbox

EBay recognised the potential of Half.com, acting swiftly to turn a competitor into a partner

Although buying the business brought Half.com into the eBay family and eliminated it as competition, this didn't change the fact that some buyers preferred the option to pay a set price for a specific product, without having to go through the bidding process. EBay responded to this by adding the 'Buy It Now' feature to selected auctions during the 2000 Christmas holiday season. Sellers could choose to include a price at which they were willing to end the auction and finalise their sale immediately. Buy It Now was so popular with both sellers and buyers that, by early 2001, a third of the listings on eBay offered it.

At that time, eBay had more than 25 million registered buyers and sellers spread around the globe, thanks to eBay-owned auction sites run out of more than half a dozen countries, including Germany, Australia and Great Britain. Such enormous growth fuelled great sales figures (in 2000, users recorded more than £3.37 billion), but it also made policing all of the auctions difficult. **Fraud** had been an occasional problem since the company's beginning, which had led to the creation of a Trust & Safety division that designed software to identify patterns associated with illegal bidding, selling counterfeit items or misrepresenting items during an auction.

By 2000, less than .01 per cent of the approximately 40 million auctions on eBay had resulted in fraud complaints. Still, it was impossible to stop some corruption from infiltrating the site. One of the worst examples had occurred just before Christmas 1998, when a man auctioned off £18,750 worth of items on eBay. He cashed all of the cheques, but never delivered the products to the buyers. When this made headlines in the American news media eBay was embarrassed. And when the *Wall Street Journal* quoted a source from the National Consumers League saying that it received 600 complaints a month about Internet fraud, many related to online auctions, eBay's stock dropped.

In 2001, the company won a crucial lawsuit that helped define its responsibilities for certain types of fraud. The suit had been brought against

As a business with international appeal, eBay soon had offices in Germany (shown here) and elsewhere.

eBay because some of the autographed sporting memorabilia that had been listed on the site was tied to a criminal operation that had allegedly **forged** autographs on millions of pounds' worth of collectibles. The **plaintiffs** argued that eBay should have to provide certificates of authenticity and prove that an item was autographed by the sports personality in his or her own hand, as other dealers in California were required to do. EBay contended that it was neither an auctioneer nor a dealer. Instead, it called itself 'the modern incarnation of the traditional newspaper classified advertisement'. A California judge agreed that eBay wasn't responsible for verifying that sellers' claims were accurate. The case was dismissed in January 2001.

In the summer of 2002, eBay completed an **acquisition** that combined the world's largest online marketplace with PayPal, the top online payment system. PayPal had been founded in November 1999 in response to shoppers' worries that their credit card numbers could be stolen if they were used to make purchases online. PayPal's **encrypted** payment system allowed people to transfer money from computer to computer without entering a credit card number for each transaction. By 2002, PayPal was handling one in every four transactions completed on eBay, even though the auction site owned a similar payment service of its own. But as PayPal's domination of the market grew, eBay decided to abandon its own service and purchase it.

This acquisition helped boost eBay's total employee count to 4,000, including engineers who kept the site running, marketing specialists and administrative support. But two key employees were missing. Omidyar had abandoned his office in the summer of 2000, giving up all day-to-day responsibilities (although he maintained the title of chairman) to help build eBay's international outlets from Paris, France. Skoll had disengaged from the business as well. The foundation of the company was shifting.

"We continue to view eBay as the best public example to date of a profitable Internet commerce model."

ANTHONY NOTO, FINANCIAL ANALYST

PayPal, which cost eBay £0.94 billion, brought growth and greater efficiency to eBay

PLANES, TRAINS AND ELVIS' WATER

At the US Republican National Convention in 2008, Sarah Palin, the governor of Alaska and a vice presidential candidate, proudly announced that she had put her state's luxury jet, purchased under the previous governor, on eBay. She didn't mention, however, that the plane never sold, and was eventually removed from the site. But airplanes have actually sold on eBay. In 2001, a Gulfstream jet sold for £3.06 million, making it the highest-priced item ever sold on the site as of 2010. Amongst the other oddities sold on eBay are a retired Monorail train carriage from Disney (£12,500) and a few tablespoons of water that had been preserved after being left in a plastic cup from which singer Elvis Presley drank in 1977 (£284). Odder still was the listing for Iceland, which was put on eBay to draw attention to the country's financial crisis in 2008. As the listing made clear, singer Bjork, a native Icelander, was 'not included'.

CHAPTER FOUR

Turning ten

Since her arrival in 1998, Whitman had quietly become the face of eBay as well as the driving force behind the company's tremendous growth. She had steered the company through the devastating 'dot-com bust' that began in 2000, when falling stock prices bankrupted many technology and web-based businesses.

EBay had come through that period intact – which Whitman attributed to the fact that, unlike most other dot-com start-ups, eBay had been profitable from the beginning.

As other web-based businesses disappeared eBay grew. In 2003, more than £12.5 billion worth of transactions took place on the site – an average of more than £436 in sales every second. The eight-year-old company's value of more than £20 billion was greater than fast-food restaurant McDonald's or aircraft manufacturer Boeing – one of the reasons eBay was ranked eighth on *Fortune* magazine's list of the 100 Fastest Growing Companies of the year.

Whitman received much of the credit for the company's rapid rise, but she humbly deflected most of it. Firstly, she pointed to the brilliance of Omidyar's idea, and to the work he and Skoll had done in launching the company. But

'EBay' is a shortened version of 'Echobay', the name Pierre Omidyar had initially preferred

she also believed that the simple formula around which eBay had been built – providing a global marketplace for the exchange of goods between individual parties – was responsible for most of the company's success. So pervasive was this thought at eBay headquarters that the saying 'a monkey could drive this train' was an established part of company jargon.

What Whitman could do that a monkey couldn't, however, was seek out opportunities for growth – including international expansion. By 2004, the company had established sites in nearly 20 countries, including India and China. At that time, almost 15 per cent of the transactions taking place on eBay involved buyers and sellers who lived in different countries; Whitman was confident this number would grow as eBay continued to expand around the globe. "I'd be surprised if that's not 50 per cent to 60 per cent 10 years from now," she said in 2005.

EBay was just marking its 10th birthday as Whitman made that bold prediction. The company invited its users – which at the time hovered around 181 million worldwide – to come celebrate at its annual user conference, eBay Live! More than 10,000 showed up at the party in San Jose, California, where they were treated to a barbecue and a private concert by the band The B-52s.

But eBay had more to celebrate in 2005 than turning 10. The company had branched out beyond its hallmark auction business with a trio of strategic acquisitions that year: Rent.com, the leading Internet listing site for rental housing in America; Shopping.com, a leader in online comparison shopping which allowed users to view prices from different retailers; and Skype, a global communications company allowing users around the world to talk to each other over the Internet.

Skype had started offering its free computer-to-computer telephone service just two years earlier. Millions of people used that service, but almost two million more also paid a small monthly fee for a Skype connection between computers and landlines or mobile phones. EBay spent £1.62 billion to bring

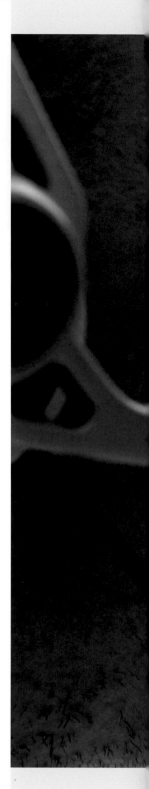

Starting in 2006, Skype enabled users with the necessary computer software and webcams to make video calls

the company into its fold – an investment that some experts saw as risky, as it didn't fit neatly within eBay's core auction and retail businesses.

This wasn't the only financial issue for eBay in 2005. In January, the company announced that it would be increasing fees for sellers in America from the standard 5 per cent on items under £15.60 to 5.25 per cent; fees for items over £15.60 increased by a quarter of a per cent as well. EBay also announced that it would begin charging buyers a fee for using the popular 'Buy It Now' feature. At the same time, news leaked that Whitman was being courted by Disney to become CEO there. She made it clear that she wasn't leaving, but eBay users reacted negatively to both the fee rises and the rumours of her departure. For the first time, **profits** dipped below expectations.

The purchase of the online ticket resale service StubHub early in 2007 provided a quick shot in the arm for eBay. By the end of the year, more than 5 million tickets to sporting events, concerts and other performances had been sold through StubHub. PayPal was also doing exceptionally well, and was the preferred method of payment for eight per cent of all online shoppers worldwide. Despite its popularity, many long-time eBay users objected to the company's new requirement that all sellers offer the option to pay with PayPal. The company explained that using PayPal helped close auctions faster because the transfer of funds happened immediately, and helped combat fraud as it was easier to track – but many users saw it as eBay's way to make more money by directing buyers and sellers towards a company-owned payment system.

The PayPal controversy marked the beginning of a change for eBay. Despite solid sales within certain divisions – including eBay Motors, which had sold more than two million passenger vehicles as of 2006 – the company's stock price started slipping, while the total number of auctions listed on the site declined, worrying even the most loyal users. After surviving the dot-com bust, eBay's unshakable hold on the market was beginning to appear fragile.

"*If you look at our track record, what we proved is that people are good. And that's pretty cool.*"

JEFF SKOLL, FORMER PRESIDENT OF EBAY

eBay Live! Berlin 27.09.2003

EBay broadened its global exposure by holding eBay Live! events in Germany and other countries

An Inconvenient Truth production team

Jeff Skoll's business plan for eBay helped turn the online auction site into one of the most successful e-commerce businesses in the world. But what he has done with the millions he made when eBay went public in 1998 might also help change the world. Skoll guided eBay's efforts to start its own philanthropic foundation in 1998 – and in 1999, he created the Skoll Foundation to invest in 'the world's most promising social entrepreneurs in order to effect lasting, positive change worldwide'. Hundreds of organisations have been honoured with the Skoll Awards for Social Entrepreneurship, including the Amazon Conservation Team and the Global Footprint Network. Skoll also founded Participant Media, a global company committed to producing films that 'inspire and compel social change'. In 2006, it produced Al Gore's Academy Award-winning global warming documentary *An Inconvenient Truth.* "This Al Gore film, whoa," Skoll said. "This movie may save the planet. That's pretty cool.

CHAPTER FIVE

Changing of the guard

Meg Whitman had said several times during her tenure at eBay that she believed a CEO should not stay at any one company more than 10 years as organizations could always benefit from the fresh ideas that new leadership offered.

And as her 10-year anniversary with the company drew nearer, it became increasingly clear to Whitman that eBay needed to reinvent itself again. So it came as no surprise when the 51-year-old announced her resignation from eBay in January 2008 – 10 years after joining the company in 1998.

Although Whitman's departure came in the midst of eBay's first real financial struggles, her decade with the company had been a prosperous and productive one. When Whitman appeared, eBay had just 30 employees – most of whom had put their own desks together and sat in old beach chairs – and boasted £2.9 million in revenue. At the time of her departure eBay employed over 15,000 people and topped £4.4 billion in revenue. "Meg's passion for all things eBay changed the world," said Omidyar, who continued as chairman of the board. "With humour, smarts [cleverness] and unflappable determination, Meg took a small, barely known online auction site and helped it become an integral part of our lives."

Meg Whitman left eBay in 2008; in 2009, she began campaigning to become governor of California

John Donahoe, who had joined eBay in 2005 as the president of eBay's Marketplaces, which handled all of the site's e-commerce, was named the next CEO. His task was to breathe new life into the company's core business: the auctions, which accounted for approximately 70 per cent of eBay's income. But before he could focus his attention on improvements Donahoe had to deal with an unexpected problem. In autumn 2008, the **economy** in America and around the world started spiralling downwards – and this time, eBay went with it.

In 2008, for the first time in the company's history, the total value of items sold on eBay's sites dropped and revenue fell. As the company's stock prices plunged to a five-year low of £11.20, Donahoe glumly announced in October that eBay would have to sack 10 per cent of its nearly 16,000 employees – the first significant job cuts the company had ever had to make.

The dismal state of the economy was only partly to blame. The **recession** had simply brought eBay's stagnant **business model** to light. As buyers and sellers had become more diverse and sophisticated, their expectations of the site had grown. They wanted the company to revisit its fee model and to offer more options for how and when they could sell their items. But instead of reacting to the requests of the people who had helped build the business from the beginning, eBay had turned its attention to acquisitions and global growth. Sellers, many of whom had built their own online 'eBay stores' on the site, had started defecting to other auction sites; buyers had begun turning to competitors such as Amazon.

In 2009, Donahoe made it clear that he wanted to woo them back. The company sold all but 30 per cent of its holdings in Skype, which had still not meshed well into the company's group of offerings, and considered dumping other irrelevant holdings as well. It modified its search engine to bring listings from sellers with higher rankings (based on buyer feedback) to the top of the results. "We have begun significant change," Donahoe said. "The eBay you knew is not the eBay we are – or the eBay we will become."

With the company soaring, John Donahoe made £6.3 million as eBay CEO in 2009

Things started to stabilise at the end of 2009. In the third **quarter**, eBay's revenue grew for the first time in more than a year. Although profit numbers were still down, Donahoe felt confident that the increase in revenue was a solid indicator that the company was rebounding. With more than 90 million users trading approximately £1,190 worth of goods each second, things were bound to get better.

For its 15th anniversary in 2010, eBay planned another gala event in San Jose, California for its users. Part of that August party was devoted to sharing upcoming plans with buyers and sellers, including the implementation of expanded loyalty programmes such as eBay Bucks, which would give buyers site credit for a percentage of every qualified purchase. But Donahoe also talked about the company's plans to evolve from a site known primarily for its auctions, to more of an online retailer poised for growth. With only five per cent of retail money spent online as opposed to in physical shops, Donahoe saw opportunity for expansion as a retailer of the products people need. "We still get referred to as an online auctioneer," he said, "but we have moved way beyond that … We need to evolve from an auctions site to an e-commerce site."

Although eBay has grown exponentially since Pierre Omidyar started it as a hobby in 1995, the business is still based on the same concept it was back then: uniting buyers and sellers in a marketplace where demand helps set the prices. And eBay's amazing growth continues – in November 2012 the company announced that it was planning to invest in a partnership with Xiu.com, a Chinese online retailer, to take advantage of the opportunities available as the world's biggest internet market, China, continues to expand.

Over the years, eBay has helped millions of people find great deals on an incredible assortment of products, and has provided a livelihood for thousands of dedicated sellers as well. Even if it's not the 'perfect online marketplace' Omidyar had originally envisioned, eBay has indeed changed the way the world shops.

> "I don't think any of us had any idea it would be so huge and encompass the whole world eventually."

LONG-TIME EBAY USER AND EMPLOYEE JIM GRIFFITH

Comedian Mario Cantone hosted a live eBay game show called 'Let's Make a Daily Deal' in 2009

GOING GREEN

When eBay opened a new corporate building on its campus in San Jose, California in spring 2008, its efforts to be good to the environment were recognised locally and nationally. The building was constructed with solar panels (upping the number on the campus to more than 3,248, which provide 18 per cent of the power for all the buildings), automatic light dimmers, low-flow taps and eco-friendly irrigation systems to water the landscaping, all of which helped it achieve LEED (Leadership in Energy and Environmental Design) Gold standards and become the greenest building in the city. But eBay was green long before that building went up. The business was built around the sale of used items that might otherwise have been tossed in landfills. "More than £62.5 billion worth of used goods have been traded on eBay," CEO John Donahoe said in 2009. "In that sense, we're the world's biggest recycler."

GLOSSARY

acquisition the purchase of one company by another

administrators the people in charge of maintaining and operating a computer system or network

bids proposed prices offered by potential buyers of an item

brand the name of a product or manufacturer; a brand distinguishes a product from similar products made by other manufacturers

business model the particular way in which a business operates, including the specific plan for how it will make money

codes the arrangements of data or instructions in a computer program that tell the computer how to operate that particular program

e-commerce the buying and selling of products and services over the Internet

economy the system of producing, distributing and consuming goods within a society

encrypted converted with a secret code, making data unintelligible to anyone not authorised to use it or not having the password to return it to its original form

entrepreneurial having the attitude or qualities of an entrepreneur, or a person who begins a new business

executive a decision-making leader of a company, such as the chairman or chief executive officer (CEO)

forged falsely reproduced signatures or other identifying characteristics to deliberately deceive another party

fraud an illegal act characterised by intentional dishonesty, hidden information or a violation of trust, usually for personal gain

Internet service provider a company that provides Internet access to the general public

philanthropic relating to charitable giving or aid intended to better other people's lives

plaintiffs people who bring a lawsuit against another person, group of people or business

profits the amount of money that a business keeps after subtracting expenses from income

public relations the practice of establishing and maintaining a favourable connection between a company and the public

quarter one of four three-month intervals that together comprise the financial year; public companies must report certain data on a quarterly basis

recession a period of decline in the financial stability of a country or society that typically includes a drop in the stock market, an increase in unemployment, and a decline in home sales

server the main computer in a network, or group of linked computers, on which shared programs and files are stored

shares the equal parts a company may be divided into; shareholders each hold a certain number of shares, or a percentage, of the company

start-ups new business ventures in their earliest stage of development

stock shared ownership in a company by many people who buy shares, or portions, or stock, hoping the company will make a profit and the stock value will increase

stock options options for employees or investors in a company to buy or sell that company's stock; stock options are often given as part of an employee's benefits package

strategic planning the process of identifying a company's long-term goals and objectives, and creating a plan to reach them

1995	Pierre Omidyar creates AuctionWeb
1996	Chris Agarpao, Jeff Skoll and Mary Lou Song join the company; Feedback Forum set-up
1997	Beanie Babies become craze on AuctionWeb; company renamed eBay
1998	Meg Whitman hired as CEO; eBay stocks made available to the public
1999	eBay suffers an outage for 22 hours
2000	eBay buys Half.com; eBay adds 'Buy It Now' feature; Omidyar moves to Paris to build eBay internationally
2002	eBay purchases PayPal service
2003	Fortune magazine names eBay number eight on the 100 Fastest Growing Companies of the year list
2005	eBay sets up Rent.com, Shopping.com, and Skype; John Donahue joins company
2007	eBay purchases StubHub
2008	Meg Whitman leaves eBay; John Donahue named CEO
2009	eBay sold 30 per cent of holdings in Skype
2010	eBay held a gala for users in San Jose, California for its 15th anniversary
2012	eBay announces partnership with Xiu.com, a Chinese online retailer, to boost its sales in the country

INDEX